NEW TRENDS IN FLOWER ARRANGEMENT

NEW TRENDS IN
FLOWER ARRANGEMENT

by Rae L. Goldson

HEARTHSIDE PRESS INCORPORATED

Publishers • New York 10016

CONTENTS

Changing Arrangements in a Changing World 9
A New Way of Thinking About Art 19
Living with Good Design 25
The New Interest in Texture 29
The Infinite Variety of Sources in Art and Arrangement
   35
"Form Follows Function" 39
"Less is More" 51
The Long History of Modern Art 55
Impressionism and Communication 59
Fantastic Art 61
Assemblage—Expressions of Environment 69
Why Junk Culture? 73
Futurism—Contemporary Emotions 75
Abstraction—Design Rather Than Subject Becomes
   Primary 77
Nature as Expressed in Contemporary Terms 81
The Simplicity of Calder's Mobiles Reflected in Modern
   Arrangements 85
Pop Art—Suggestions for Future Arrangements 87
Perception and the Arranger 89
New Rules for the Advanced Arranger 91
Flower Arrangement as a Creative Art Expression 107
Index 117

NEW TRENDS IN FLOWER ARRANGEMENT

CHANGING ARRANGEMENTS
IN A CHANGING WORLD

Ten years ago, in *Contemporary Flower Arrangement,* I made the statement that flower arrangement, as an art, had been changing. If that was true more than a decade ago, it is even more true today, when flower arrangement reflects the tremendous changes that have taken place not only in the world around us, but also in our way of looking at that world.

The new rules in the *Handbook for Flower Shows* (National Council of State Garden Clubs, Inc.) allow much greater latitude and hence much more creativity for flower arrangers. They are a consequence of a new view of art which finds beauty in what could once have been deemed unlikely places; in fact, in the new view of art all the old rules are turned upside down.

It would have been impossible for flower arranging not to change when everything about us is changing. Space exploration, telestar communication, and computerization have widened the possibilities for man, and these vast technological advances have altered the way we think about the smaller events and objects around us. Trends in fashions, in travel, the way we eat, education for our children, entertainment—all have changed, even in these last ten years, and are continuing to change.

1. So many containers are hackneyed and boring but this one from America House (in New York City) is fresh and lovely. The lid could be used as an accessory.

9

2. Some arrangers feel, mistakenly, that all modern work is abstract. Here the liberties taken with scale—note how the linear material towers over the figure of Pan—mark this work as modern in feeling, but it has no abstract quality at all.

3. Here is another transitional design. Modern abstractionists do not use sentimental figures, considering them mawkish and trite. This is expressive of natural scenery. Materials: Natural wood branch with brown dock, orange dahlias, peony leaves, wood base, and carved figure of antelope as accessory.

4. (Opposite) The work of many modern artists, for example Dali and Seurat, portrays a love of precision. Details are shown with minute exactitude, and in this arrangement, with its sharply focused twiggy lines which invite the eye to stop and explore and examine each crevice, a similar predilection for details is evident. This design is naturalistic and expressive. Materials: A dried stalk of coconut spray with dock and orange chrysanthemums, pieces of bog oak at the base, and a carved figure of a whittler.

5. Can you imagine objects more foreign to traditional flower arrangement than this air filter from a car, a dried artichoke flower, and a grouping of dried mullein? This non-realistic abstraction has a strong, masculine look — reminiscent of a piece of machine-age sculpture in welded iron.

6. You must understand that there are many new trends in our art, and often they overlap each other and work of the past as well. One new trend is to use materials formerly unknown in flower arrangements, in this case strips of aluminum. They are, however, arranged in a traditional design, somewhat similar to the wisteria in Plate 2, but the aluminum has a more baroque, more formal quality in keeping with the dignified black container. Blue hydrangeas and one large philodendron leaf to balance them, placed on a diagonal in the neck of the container, follow the general pattern of the aluminum strips.

7. Although our art is under-
going many changes, we continue to be aware of the in-
fluences which ancient ages
have had on modern architecture, gardening, and interior
décor. Hence many new-trend
arrangements express a pe-
riod feeling too. This one,
which finds its inspiration in
the strength and massiveness
of historic Spain, suggests its
characteristic iron and delicate scrollwork. It is five feet
high. Materials: Dried leaves
of the century plant, painted
black on one side, red on the
other; aluminum strips; red
dahlias and cut philodendron
leaves; concrete broken from
the side of a garden bench
used as container.

8. (Opposite) Expressing the new trend—largeness in scale, richness in detail, sculptured form. Materials: Driftwood, coconut spathe, two dried aralia leaves and orange day lilies.

9. We continue to link the old world with the new one, using materials typical of each. Here a wine bottle slipped through an air filter holds sheaths of the banana tree, two roses, and aucuba foliage. The force of the circle balances the tall slender lines; the small circle of the flowers brings transition.

A NEW WAY OF
THINKING ABOUT ART

Perhaps what is most important to the flower arranger is the new way of thinking about art. Flower arranging as an art is intimately concerned with this. For example, when the Museum of Modern Art considers a large pile of squashed and arranged automobile fenders painted in raw enamels to be a genuine piece of modern sculpture, it behooves us to try to understand what is going on in the art world even though we need not translate every new trend into flower arrangement. We can no longer expect that knowledge of the traditional design principles alone will give us an understanding of art. Today painting and sculpture take many forms, and are rooted in the complex, violent, sometimes vulgar, dynamic and affecting fabric of our present-day lives. What we used to consider ugly now often seems beautiful to us because it is made up of, and comments on, the elements of our time.

10. Is it art? is asked about many modern works. Similarly, is it a flower arrangement? could be the question here. In our new way of thinking the stalk of an onion plant has as much inherent interest, as much claim to use in a flower arrangement, as a long-stemmed rose. Foliage of yucca, hosta and dieffenbachia, and one large dahlia, are included.

19

11. Here strips of spathe take on the quality of modern urban materials, specifically the smoothness of steel and aluminum bands which are included. Three chartreuse Fuji chrysanthemums and a green aralia leaf are the other elements.

12. (Opposite, left) Here the coconut spathe strips are used as a fluid sculptural medium with two strelitzia flowers and one aralia leaf in a heavy brown textured container on a round base.

13. (Opposite, right) Using the same container, the coconut spathe strips were placed in a nonrepresentational abstraction expressing pure design. The lilies soften and emphasize the simplicity of the spathes.

14. Few materials used in a grand scale, and the unusual way-off-center placement of the chrysanthemum and aralia leaf against the Scotch broom in the container, all bespeak the untraditional design. The lines cascading down one side soften the hard lines of the container.

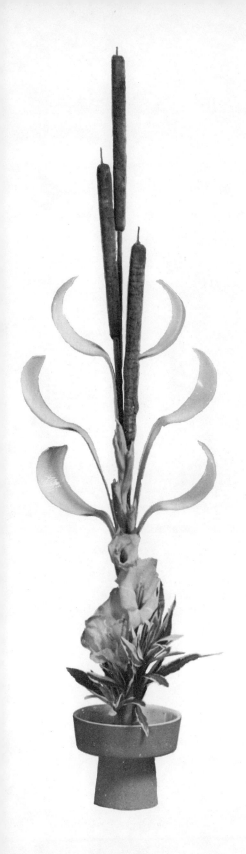

15. There is a concession to traditional arranging in the grouping of gladioli and oleander foliage but abstraction comes with the addition of the symmetrical cactus spoons. They seem to have been borne out of the organic softness of the flowers at the base, their shining orderliness offset by the roughness of the thrusting cattails. The tall lines dwarf the container, but the grouping of solid forms well above the neck of the container exerts a steadying influence.

16. Flower arrangement has been influenced by modern design but has influenced it too, as you can see from these contemporary ceramic weed holders (America House).

LIVING WITH GOOD DESIGN

At the same time, like the fine arts, flower arrangements go beyond the competition hall and the gallery. In our homes, and the places where we gather socially, they serve a purpose. They are meant to enhance, to amuse, to please by the way they occupy the space in which they are placed, and even to communicate some deeper meaning through symbolism, line and color. Modern flower arrangements, like modern art, can do all this — through wit, through humor, through boldness in the choice of materials and containers, through craftsmanship in technique, and through an academic knowledge of such design elements as balance, harmony, color and line.

Today we live intimately with good design, and for this reason, too, we look for good design in flower arrangements. Our clothing, the packaging, the architecture around us vary from spoofs on "Pop Art" and "Op Art" to a near-literal translation of the modern abstractionists, Leger and Mondrian. The cereal box at the breakfast table, the format of the daily paper, the Op Art dresses on display in a local little shop, the way in which the suburban railroad station is painted—the everyday scenes and objects from the time we start our day to the Late Late Show when we watch Surrealist commercials and films in our bedrooms upholstered in flat tones and Op Art designs of contemporary decorating—all have been influenced by modern painting and sculpture.

25

17. (Opposite, left) In modern floral art, it's hard to separate the weeds from the flowers. Fuzzy cattails give evidence of the modern absorption with linear quality, rather than with flowers or leaves *per se.* The container, a dried gourd, has three openings. Small orange-yellow chrysanthemums are in two of the openings.

18. (Opposite, right) Reminiscent of the predilection of modern architects to offset the somber mass of concrete by grillwork, this container (made from radiator mesh) is set on a dark base, the lacy Fuji chrysanthemums contrasting with cut palmetto foliage.

19. Cattails again, but this time only three, rather than three different groupings, with less textural effect. Again in contrast, this container is heavily textured. Originally a smooth pottery, it was covered with a coat of white shellac, dipped in coarse sand, and left to dry. Orange day lilies and cactus leaf are the other materials.

THE NEW INTEREST IN TEXTURE

In modern paintings and in modern sculpture there is a new interest in *textures*—in contrasts of materials. Assemblages, groups of familiar objects are brought together by the artist. Sculpture is created in "mixed media"—that is, using not only the conventional materials of plaster, marble, wood or stone but also fabrics, mesh, plaster or wood with veneers of printed or painted canvas or paper, and even baked dough (a material for which one Pop artist is noted). Metal sculpture is forged out of intentionally roughened metals in jagged sections.

Flower arrangement echoes this new interest in texture and the use of contrasts in materials. We combine plant materials of silken sheen and sheets of translucent plastic with elemental, forceful metal or stone; eroded, rusty metal with velvet flowers and leaves; and we look for materials of spiky, many-faceted surfaces which will catch the light and appear different to the eye when seen at different angles.

20. A contrast of lacy, delicate materials with those that look solid and bulky offers the textural feeling often exhibited in modern art forms. This design is essentially Spanish in mood and color—but the new trend is eclectic. Materials: Cattails, skeletonized cactus, aucuba leaves and red carnations. The container was made from two cans covered with white shellac and grit, then sprayed black.

29

21. Again a contrast of textures. Note, too, how unused spaces— or voids—become as important as the filled spaces. Materials: Scotch broom, bent and twisted to create the line, aralia leaves, persimmon-red dahlias in a pottery container on a base of three Japanese lacquered boards.

22. (Opposite) Gnarled wood, striated coconut spathe, pimpled circles of osage oranges, jagged edges of aralia leaf, looped and pointed dracaena, and succulent mullein rosette all demonstrate today's lively interest in textured surfaces.

23. A flat, roughly textured container, and large open-faced composite flower are the essence of primitive simplicity, good opposition for the subtly sophisticated form of the sinuous coconut spathe.

24. Texture, texture, texture—expressed in many sizes, shapes and forms. The curled form on the table is a fantastic creation of skeletal-like fingers extended from a malignant-looking hand.

THE INFINITE VARIETY OF SOURCES IN ART AND ARRANGEMENT

Today's art has another message for the flower arranger—the range of materials that are worthy of the arranger's attention are infinite. The artist no longer says one subject or treatment is worthy of his attention while another is too commonplace or vulgar for this attention. At one extreme this is what Andy Warhol is saying when he carefully paints facsimiles of Campbell Soup cans; it is also what modern sculptors are expressing when they make constructions of inexpensive materials — straw, wire mesh, cork — that are nevertheless expressive of volume and spatial manipulation.

In flower arrangement this may be interpreted as meaning that roses and gladioli are no more worthy of appreciation than the most common wilding or roadside wanderer and that as containers, a Baccarat crystal or expensive ceramic may not offer more esthetic opportunities than do a rusty crankcase from an old auto, or a discarded spring.

I would like to stress that to me the important thing is never the rareness or beauty of the materials and containers I use, but the effect derived from the whole arrangement. Mullein, a dried artichoke flower, an air filter from a car may add up to an abstraction that has dignity, even a kind of regality.

Constantly searching for unusual and attractive materials in one's immediate surroundings, one begins to be far more

25. African carvings have had a tremendous influence on abstract art. The unusual container so oddly reminiscent of Negro sculpture has been combined with geraniums, bold cattails and leaves sprayed black, producing a work of primitive simplicity and directness, qualities which typify African design.

35

26. Spoofing the traditional harvest arrangement a "cornucopia" of driftwood hangs from an orange container holding dahlias, orange lilies and fake grapes.

conscious of the form, line and texture of everyday objects. The result is a sharpened sense of your surroundings, a new perception of the value of everything you see.

Because, too, in modern design and modern art there is a feeling of surprise, of wit, in the mixing of the formal and the informal, the elaborate and the simple, the expensive brass and the rough wood, flower arrangers today feel free to combine exotic and formal flowers with humble containers—or vice versa—or to combine exotic flowers with simple wild flowers, whatever is most expressive to achieve an idea or mood.

There is a general cross-pollinization of art and design today which affects flower arranging too. What is being created in the artist's studio is soon echoed in designs for fabrics, furniture, accessories and table settings. The flower arranger is a designer, too, who is bound to want to design in such a way that her arrangements will be at home in contemporary settings. To arrange in this contemporary idiom one has to be bold in so far as the usual rules for competition are concerned. The National Council of State Garden Clubs recognizes this when it includes "Free Style" and "Abstract Arrangements" under the types of contemporary artistic design allowed today.

Thus you may now follow the dictates of "good design" created "outside the established geometric patterns," according to the *Handbook*. In abstract design, for example, less attention is given to focal point or center of interest. Structural aids are sometimes visible rather than hidden. Even the pinholder may be exposed. We are not concerned about covering the lip of the container.

36

27. The form and texture of the black pitcher and its obvious visual relationship to the strelitzia leaves dictated this design in which container and plant material seem extensions of each other, with anthuriums for dramatic interest.

28. (Above) Modern materials, modern techniques of flower arrangement and a classic container produce a work which looks "new trend" but is not abstract. Tan and brown spathes were soaked in warm water, then bent to shape. Combined with orange century lilies and aralia leaves, they are shown against yellow textured silk.

29. (Right) The search for new kinds of containers led to the use of a toy bowling pin which was improved by the addition of texture.

"FORM FOLLOWS FUNCTION"

Such a casting off of the rules which we have followed for so many years is not anarchy—a flouting of rules just to be different. Rather, this too has roots in modern art and architecture. For example, exposing the mechanics of the arrangements, making them part of the design, employs one of the most venerable rules of modern design—*Form Follows Function*. In a modern flower arrangement (as in a multi-story building by Mies Van der Rohe, where the structural skeleton is exposed and made part of the design), the functional parts, the mechanics, lend the total arrangement strength and interest.

30. Integration is the important word here, for the base and part of the plant material function as integral parts of each other. The half-abstract bird made of driftwood, two skeletonized cactus leaves sprayed black, and three Fuji chrysanthemums are lofted on a stand made of various pieces of bamboo.

39

31. This study in black and white was made for a flower show at the New York Horticultural Society. Since the abstract arranger feels free to paint plant materials (and painted material was permitted) the wisteria branch was sprayed black, and the aspidistra leaf was sprayed black on one side and white underneath. Two white chrysanthemums were included. A white container, black inside, was placed on a black wooden stand. The textured background fabric was grey, with black and white flecks.

32. (Opposite) Planned for an Easter flower show. Since Medieval days, the lily, emblem of purity, has been associated with the Madonna, but this arrangement takes on a modern frivolity by the addition of more contemporary plant materials and the use of an undefined shape crudely molded from clay to represent the Mother.

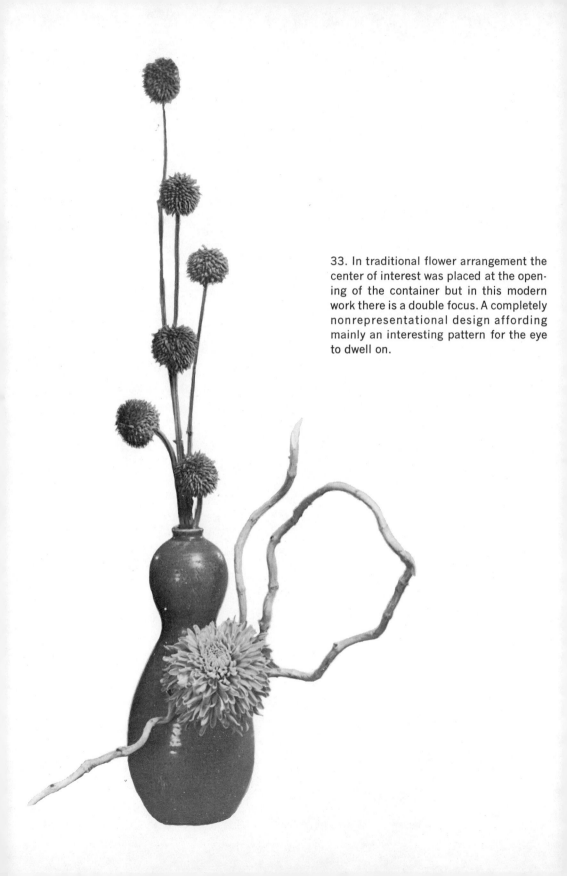

33. In traditional flower arrangement the center of interest was placed at the opening of the container but in this modern work there is a double focus. A completely nonrepresentational design affording mainly an interesting pattern for the eye to dwell on.

34. To express a nightmare for a flower show piece—driftwood with strange contortions, a thin coconut spathe, leaves of dracaena and aralia and bright orange lilies make a forceful composition.

35. (Left) The theme of this expressive design was Sea Serpent, visualized with a coiled car spring holding a writhing piece of driftwood encircling red dahlias and aralia leaves. More of the plant material sprawled placidly at the base.

36. (Below) The off-center arrangement has been influenced by modern sculpture. No attempt has been made to conceal the mechanics.

37. Here is an interpretation of Mondrian's first abstraction, derived from nature and based on curving lines delicately balanced in advancing and receding thrusts and checks.

38. The figurines are an abstract ceramic of a bullfighter and bull in black and red. Two strips of narrow coconut spathe painted black outside and red inside are used with dark dracaena leaves and brilliant red carnations.

39. (Opposite) This is essentially a Futuristic arrangement. Plant materials, base and accessory figure all suggest motion.

40. Hardware cloth made into a tube holds the base of a heavy branch in a cupholder, placed in a lovely odd-shaped woven boat container. White chrysanthemums and mahonia suggest the complex forms of nature.

41. Use of materials at hand, as in the case of the boat, is implicit in many modern inventive assemblages.

42. (Right) In the Spanish manner. Skeletonized cactus leaves sprayed black represent Spanish lace and celosia in brilliant red is the toreador's cape. Black cattails carry out the Hispanic theme. Again as in most good assemblages a few materials can dramatically stand for entire systems of thought and manners.

"LESS IS MORE"

Another basic tenet of modern design is *Less is More*—which means that the fewer meaningless decorations and ornamentations, and the fewer the materials used, the more the design or work of art has to offer. Picasso, for example, has always been fond of displaying his ability to do much with little. An illustration is his "sculpture" of a bull's head composed of a bicycle seat and handle bars. Such a piece displays humor, spontaneity and an ability to improvise and invent with limited means.

This is the kind of use of material contemporary flower arrangers have in mind when they speak of inspiration coming from the material itself.

We must develop this restraint of "less is more" and learn to use only that which is important to the design. If only one or two flowers are sufficient, do not spoil the effect by adding more!

43. Again the "less is more" principle is exemplified here. There is only one kind of plant material, but note the different shapes to which it has been altered: spiral, diagonal, curve and bend.

51

44. (Opposite) Only Kaffir corn is used here, with its own foliage, but the smallness of the pattern of the tips slows the eye and contrasts with the smooth sweep of stalk which carries the eye quickly down, thereby creating variety which is necessary for design interest. This is a naturalistic expressive design.

45. This very simple design carries with it a feeling that the space has been well filled, a quality missed by many a more elaborate design. Osage oranges of different sizes were raised on stems with oleander foliage at the point where container and material merge. (An interesting departure from the usual design in which the pattern is line and the fill-in material is mass.)

46. Kaffir corn again, this
time only a few stalks, but the
design interest arises from
one tiny factor — the crossed
stalk.

THE LONG HISTORY OF MODERN ART

The purpose of this book is to help you to work, as does any modern craftsman or designer, with an understanding of the principles of modern art and design. Modern painting and sculpture have been in the making for at least a century, and they draw upon such sources as ancient civilizations and even prehistoric sculpture and cave drawings for inspiration.

Usually, however, modern painting is said to have begun with the Impressionists who experimented with light and color, trying to get the feeling of nature by breaking color into small pieces.

Modern art can scarcely be said to have travelled a straight road since then. It has taken many strange paths. There have been leaps ahead, steps backward, self-destructive trends which reduce all art to chaos.

The most popular movements at the present time, and the movements which are having an effect upon flower arrangement, are those of Pop Art, Op Art and non-representational Abstraction, particularly that expressed in mobile and stabile (non-moving) constructions in sculpture.

Before discussing these recent movements, let us very briefly talk about the older trends that have influenced the new look.

47. An attempt to interpret modern sculpture which is involved not only with the solid design but also with the space it encloses and the space enclosed in it. Materials: Frothy feathery white pampas grass, loops of pussy willow painted red, two roses and foliage in a pottery container with a tear drop opening.

55

48. To balance the heavy black form of the container, free-form loops of wisteria, painted white, are interwoven with a white dahlia and a grouping of three tips of mullein. One heavy loop of aralia shrub painted black gives added weight where needed.

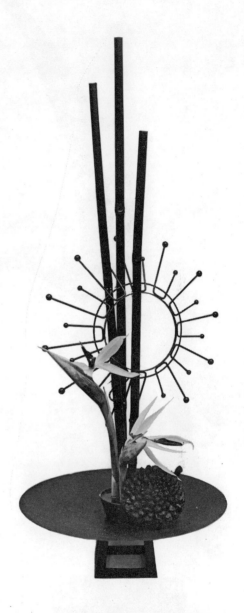

49. An assemblage interpreting the sunflower. It includes the fruit of the pandanus, strelitzia, the frame of a clock and a plow disc on a wooden stand. Note the partly exposed cup-holder.

50. A semi-abstraction. Here the bird carved from driftwood is recognizable; in an abstract design a symbol of light, rather than a realistic shape, would have been used. Bright red gladioli are set high above the opening of the container, and no attempt has been made to camouflage the opening with a flower, leaf, moss, etc., as would have been done in traditional work.

IMPRESSIONISM AND COMMUNICATION

Impressionism (founded by the two great masters, Renoir and Seurat) was partly a response to the camera with its ability to capture the surface appearance of things. But it was also the start toward paintings which were not so much pictorial as they were an attempt to paint a feeling, a mood, a concept.

We are now in the process of rediscovering the English painter, Turner, who although he died one hundred and fifteen years ago, left us pictures which seem to have been painted yesterday. What is contemporary about his paintings is that he, like the Impressionists, saw the world as light and color, but in addition he saw that paintings could be an "independent imaginative function." The essayist, Hazlitt, we are told, called Turner's paintings "pictures of nothing."

In flower arranging, we are now frequently concerned with such paintings of nothing. That is to say we are not trying to reproduce or rearrange nature, or to preserve it in an attractive manner, but rather to express *ideas of the mind* and to *communicate* them through the medium of flower arrangement.

Impressionism, and the work that followed it, has had another meaning for us. We now realize that we need no longer follow set rules but must use whatever is best for us in order to arrive at a piece that does communicate, whether that communication is a mood or an idea.

51. This attempts to communicate a personal feeling about the speed and restlessness of modern highways and their endless turnoffs. Pandanus leaves with white lines and cycas palm curled around itself were arranged in a black asymmetrical container.

59

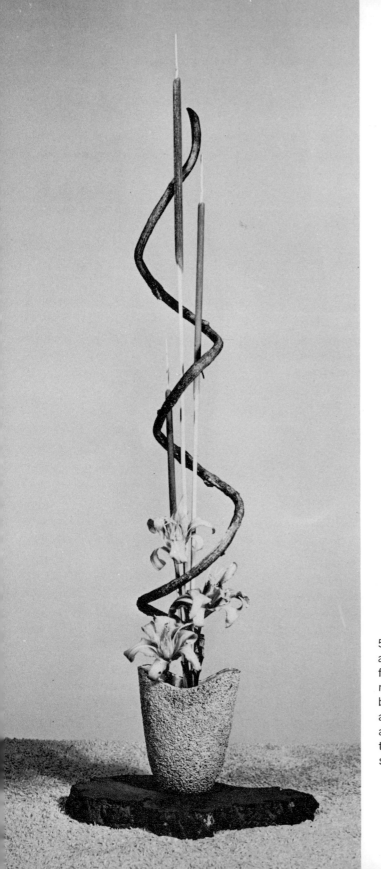

52. To symbolize growth and aspiration the spiral was the form chosen for this arrangement, executed with a spiral branch of wisteria, woven around pencil thin cattails and orange day lilies in a textured container the color of sand.

FANTASTIC ART

Among the movements that followed Impressionism and which, it seems to me, have influenced the eventual path of flower arrangement, were those of Fantastic Art, Dadaism and Surrealism. All of these were a reaching out on the part of the artists for a means of jolting the viewer into a startling experience of seeing something in a new way, the way of the artist's own dream world or imagination. Familiar objects were put in unfamiliar situations; unfamiliar situations or objects were made to seem familiar and commonplace. Fur-lined tea cups, bird cages filled with sugar cubes, eyes floating in a blue cloud-filled sky, Magritte's apples and roses straining the walls of an otherwise empty room, Dali's melting telephones and dripping watches hanging from trees—all these perhaps were not meant to be Freudian symbols and nightmares as much as they were meant to say "Don't take the world around you for granted!"

Flower arrangement has little outwardly in common with such wild leaps of the imagination, but for generations flower arrangement has rigidly adhered to strict rules, some of which came from the Japanese, and for us to break away from the old prescribed paths into new directions was just as startling at first as were the new symbols and ideas of the Surrealist painters.

61

53. In the search for synonyms for Surrealism, one is tempted to use such words as fantastic, disturbing, dreamlike, mysterious, wild or to mention the poetic imagery of Rimbaud, the writings of Freud, the obsessive paintings of de Chirico. This design has a quality common to all Surrealist work, fantasy, expressed in flower arranging terms. The bird, carved by the author, is another example of the need for the contemporary arranger to be a craftsman. If a flower arranger were to do an interpretation of Coleridge's "The Rime of the Ancient Mariner" with its huge albatross might it not look something like this? Materials: Bird carved from natural wood raised on pussy willow stem, coconut spathe, Kaffir corn, dried artichoke flower.

54. Peacock feathers have been cut to stress the eyes thus giving this arrangement the tone of Pop Art, a quality enhanced by the dark base which seems to float the eyes and lashes. Materials: Peacock feathers, hydrangea flower, cut philodendron leaf, rough textured container.

55. A most Surrealistic approach to arrangement, this demonstrates the ability of the designer to find in nature (or to adapt as in the skeletonized effect of the sea fan) materials to express any imaginative concept. The arrangement seems to flow in one line from the ceramic fish. Materials: Cut Easter palm in a fantail pattern, sea fan, pink bromeliad flowers, cut philodendron leaf, a ceramic fish and iridescent coal-black mineral at the base.

56. The fantasy displayed here is akin to the early Surrealist paintings and sculptures in which the work had more than one level of meaning. One can look at this and see driftwood and plant materials in a pleasant design. Or one can look again and see a playful animal with waving tail. With such humor, the comtemporary arranger looks at materials and accessories before commencing to unite several elements. Materials: Animal carved from driftwood, grouping of Easter palm sprayed black, strelitzia and aralia leaf, sea fan, red carnations.

57. Both composition and choice of material suggest the stuff of dreams, the unreal world of Surrealism and Dadaism. The voids composed by the hanging wood are essential to the success of the design. Materials: Two cattails, sea fan, two large yellow-to-orange chrysanthemums, and natural wood.

58. The circle design of the Mexican vase draws the eye to the colorful daisies and they become large and over-real as in Surrealist painting. The date spray was soaked in warm water, bent and trimmed and used with peony leaves. Strongly primitive in feeling.

59. (Opposite) There is something of the dream world in this design too. Materials: Easter palm with a fishtail pattern, a rosette of mullein looming extra-large, and ranunculus placed rather unnaturally so that they appear in profile, rather than head-on as is common in traditional arrangement.

ASSEMBLAGE—EXPRESSIONS
OF ENVIRONMENT

When we take a piece of junk, a miniature figure, a dried plant or driftwood form, and then combine it with a container and, perhaps, living flowers, we are engaging in one of the most popular expressions of contemporary art—assemblage.

Originally, the Dadaists, Picasso, Braque, Juan Gris, and others did create assemblages that were still paintings — pieces of fabric, theatre stubs, newsprint, magazine clippings, were pasted on the canvas, fitted together like pieces in a puzzle or overlapped, to make an abstraction, or semi-abstract "painting."

But then there were the free-standing, sculpture-like assemblages. These included "ready-mades" — objects which the artists found interesting and esthetic enough in themselves to need nothing more for exhibition purposes than to be given a catalog number and, perhaps, be placed on a pedestal. Typical was Marcel Duchamp's "Bottle Dryer" — a brass series of six circles, successively growing smaller, and rhythmically spiked with prongs for the glasses to dry upon. Actually this homely, functional object for French restaurants can be conceived of as a linear study of circles and upward thrusting prongs, and, looked at in this way it is very like the lines we attempt in contemporary arrangements.

Another artist, Robert Indiana, uses iron and wood wagon wheels in assemblages that are much like several contemporary arrange-

60. Assemblages. *The Handbook for Flower Shows* defines an assemblage in part as a "creation of great imagination composed of diverse elements." The key word in this definition is no doubt "diverse" meaning dissimilar and varied objects, which we take to mean objects not usually incorporated in flower arrangements. In this design which no doubt qualifies as an assemblage, the wagon wheel suggests the charm of rural things, the simplicity of olden days. Nostalgic symbols are often used in modern art by Dadaists and assemblers. Materials: An iron wheel on a stand with a branch of magnolia, privet branches, purple iris and mullein rosette.

69

ments I have seen. I had arrived at much the same sort of arrangement myself, without being aware of his work. A representative Indiana assemblage is called "Moon." It consists of a wood beam, painted with big white circles and with the word Moon stencilled in white at the top. Along two sides of the rectangular beam are the wheels.

What are we trying to express about our environment, about our time in history, when we seek out "junk" or free-for-the-taking material for our arrangements—springs of old clocks, rusty wheels, driftwood, eroded stones; or when we choose materials that are so far from the traditional roses and gladioli—fungus, wild milkweed pods, cattails, pitted osage oranges or dried gourds?

61. In this assemblage, a black metal clock frame symbolizes the sun, with a bird in flight to suggest the abstract idea of motion. Purple iris, aucuba leaves and several pieces of bamboo are used with a driftwood flight symbol.

62. This is an assemblage in the truest sense. In it materials from widely separated sources — man-made metal rings, bamboo, Fuji chrysanthemums and a spray of green aucuba — are bound together. The resulting expression is one of airiness and delicacy and yet of clear-cut force.

WHY JUNK CULTURE?

This is the question asked of modern composite art. Why "junk culture"? Why seek out objects that are pitted and eroded, the metal tools and junk covered with rust, the barn posts that have been used and weathered, welded nuts and bolts and old pieces of steel, discarded newspapers, keys, the limbs of mannequins, etc.?

First, there is the subject already discussed —the emphasis on the beauty and worth in what was formerly held to be distasteful and valueless, what has been described as an "attention to negative values." We find, for example, a new beauty and strength in the sharp silhouette and massive form of the cattail. The assembler finds the same value in the inherent sculptural strength of, say, an ordinary monkey wrench.

Then the choice of rusty, pitted, corroded objects suggests the passage of time, the battering of elements, the brutality of nature and life, and man's ability to survive, whether in an urban setting or a rural one. Also, many of the objects of modern arrangement and modern art are deliberately urban, another break with the past. The angularity and sharpness, the uncompromising strength of some arrangements, and much modern sculpture, as well as the deliberate choice of massive, metallic-looking materials, suggest the city.

73

63. "Found" objects, particularly those that are commonplace, are used by modern sculptors, and reassembled in formal designs. The counterpart in flower arrangement is to take cones (here, of Cedrus Atlanticus), pods, fungus, a tree log (as container), some wild plants (wild honeysuckle)—all objects found in the forests and woods— and utilize their inherent delicacy of color, textural interest and pattern to make an arresting arrangement.

64. A current trend is to recognize the relevance of humor.
There is something comic
about this design. Does it car-
icature an animal with a stuck-
up tail and slightly bowed
legs? Is there any significance
in the use of the brick raised
on bamboo stems, like modern buildings cantilevered
over a plaza, or is the whole
composition an attempt to
make something out of junk?

FUTURISM—CONTEMPORARY EMOTIONS

One of the early art movements that has had an effect upon flower arrangement was Futurism. This was an attempt to show emotions and responses to issues and environment in a passionate way. The subjects of the Futurists, in sculpture and painting, were the speed of airplanes and automobiles, the psychological effect of the world around us, the power of light. To do this, they used, in sculpture, a great multiplicity of materials, glass, wood, cardboard, iron, cement, horsehair, leather, cloth, mirrors, etc.

Many contemporary arrangements are extremely Futuristic in style. When we try to communicate the wonder of space exploration, the feeling of flight and soaring, the weightlessness and free-fall concepts in flower arrangement, we quite naturally attempt the projecting "lines of force" that the Futurists used, and like them we attempt to escape from the materiality of masses, dissolving the materials we use into several fragments and images.

One result has been the abandonment of the traditional Hogarth curve in design for the more dynamic parabola and other "moving" lines, such as the Wave. The parabola, in particular, is described as representative of the space age because missile flights follow a parabolic path. In designing an arrangement with a parabolic curve, one remembers that it is symmetrical about a vertical axis, and never closes no matter how far it is extended.

65. Futurism is no longer an influence on modern painting but its attempt to communicate speed, motion, and energy lingers in the flower arranger's world. Materials: Inverted peeled hydrangea branches with palm leaves and cocoa fiber, red flowers and fungus.

75

66. Purism, like Futurism an early offshoot of Cubism, is its exact opposite, since Futurism expressed passionate behavior and Purism—from which this arrangement derives—is essentially intellectual. It is constructed around simple geometric forms and makes no attempt to communicate an emotion. Materials: Wisteria, strelitzia leaves, echeveria.

ABSTRACTION—DESIGN RATHER THAN SUBJECT BECOMES PRIMARY

Another direction taken by both sculpture and painting which has influenced flower arrangement greatly was that of *abstraction.* Abstract flower arrangement, as abstract fine art, takes many forms, but in all of them the emphasis is on the design rather than the subject matter.

One kind of abstraction in flower arrangement is that which is completely nonrepresentational. The arrangement does not mean anything spiritual or emotional. Perhaps it is mechanical or scientific, but it is an exercise, without personal feeling, a composition in which the plant materials, the containers, the accessories are selected for what they will bring to the whole in dots, lines, planes, masses, forms, and color and texture. The blocky containers we like to use enhance this feeling of the solid, cubistic modern.

Another aspect of abstraction is represented by the familiar portraits painted by Picasso in which the features of the face are rearranged. The abstract artist takes personal liberties with what he sees. He breaks up and reassembles familiar objects. Similarly we feel free to distort reality by having our plant material take new shapes, by bending and twisting, cutting, skeletonizing and even painting plant materials in a way that has little relationship to the natural forms.

67. When you look at the main body of this design, it is easy to see the comparison to Cubist art, with its emphasis on forms and only forms, which was the beginning of abstraction. This arrangement bears little or no resemblance to arrangements of the past. It is a simple exercise in abstraction in which a sturdy flower-like form contains four uneven lines which pull the eye upward, offset by three sculptural forms which carry the eye in and around.

77

68. The abstract flower arranger ignores the obvious — in this case the obvious neck of the container—and places her design-elements (three branches of day lilies, one leaf, one strelitzia) where they will best serve her design purpose.

69. The loops of steel attached to the bamboo, the way-off-center placement of the cut philodendron leaf, the container with two different openings, mark the abstract assemblage arrangement.

70. This arrangement has the lush quality of the jungle, with its exotic materials expressive of things outside ordinary experience.

NATURE AS EXPRESSED IN CONTEMPORARY TERMS

Traditionally flower arranging has been conceived of as bright masses of color, the essence of a riotous summer garden brought into the house. For this reason it is sometimes hard to understand the earthy, somber tones of some modern arrangements, as well as the use of dried materials, and "shapeless" pottery and driftwood containers.

But modern artists have been greatly influenced by nature—by the palette of earth tones, by the organic free-form or flowing shapes in nature, and by the complexities of texture and surface design in nature. The sculptors who use an acetylene torch and metal to achieve the irregular textures and lines seen in natural forms are perhaps most close to the contemporary arranger in spirit. We use various spiky plant materials—dried ball thistle, Kaffir corn, dried branches and driftwood, Scotch broom and pineapples and artichokes, among others, to get this effect.

Often plant materials have a weird resemblance to abstract sculpture, sculpture which is only distantly representational. Typical of this are the cypress knees I sprayed white and set "facing" one another in an arrangement given scale and rich color by yellow-orange chrysanthemums at their base.

71. This Impressionistic arrangement has the typical shimmering atmospheric quality, a sense of broken tone, plus the feeling that in the next moment the scene might change as the wind shifted. Much of this is due to the fluidity of the Scotch broom, used here with the sunny yellow chrysanthemums, and a dried coconut spathe raised on an inverted wooden bowl.

81

72. The cypress knees, painted white, have an abstracted likeness to human forms, and thus this design assumes the posture of abstract sculpture. Aralia leaves, cut philodendron leaf and two large brilliant chrysanthemums are the other materials.

73. Things are not what they seem! Beautiful flowers turn out to be vegetables. Here are artichokes, cut squash and kale, with loops of dracaena leaves.

THE SIMPLICITY OF CALDER'S MOBILES REFLECTED IN MODERN ARRANGEMENTS

Alexander Calder's mobiles and stabiles have exerted a large influence on flower arranging. The *stabiles* (non-moving compositions) came first and used strong blues, reds and blacks which showed up strikingly against the whitened wires and white bases of his compositions. In flower arrangements we use these bold simple patterns connected by alternating mass and line, and the simple flat colors are striking in arrangements.

Plate 98 is a stabile which gives the *illusion* of motion and yet is stationary. This is, of course, quite different from the mobile which must have the quality of movement.

Calder's mobiles which have been imitated even in the nursery sometimes have motors to give animals and shapes the movements of animals and objects in nature. More often they are so balanced and hung that the slightest movement of air causes animation. Like Henry Moore, whose sculpture is often based on natural shapes, Calder's inspiration comes from nature, from lumps of wood, pieces of bone, the shape of a whale, beach pebbles.

74. This is a linear sculpture in which, as in a Calder stable, the elements are alternating line and mass, and simple flat colors. Three chartreuse Fuji chrysanthemums and green aucuba leaves are contained in a converted gooseneck lamp.

85

75. Compare the forceful thrusting quality of the design with the delicacy of the preceding one to see why it is expressive of masculinity.

POP ART—SUGGESTIONS FOR FUTURE ARRANGEMENTS

Pop Art which has been so much in the public consciousness for the last few years, like its earlier counterparts Dadaism and Surrealism, has not had a direct translation in arranging, as has abstract sculpture, for example. We are governed more by the principles of assemblage where the objects that are brought together have a coherence (even though that coherence may derive from pairing opposites). We do not simply throw together conglomerations nor are we interested in commenting on the trivial aspects of the commercial world, as do the Pop Artists who reproduce as works of art mass displays of soup cans or Brillo packages, or paint enlarged copies of Batman or other comic strips.

Nevertheless we should recognize in Pop Art the humor and wit, as in Picasso and Calder, for example, and appreciate that the viewer is supposed to be visually, if not emotionally, surprised. Thus Pop Artists construct refrigerators which open to interiors of dripping paint and whirring motors or larger-than-life freestanding (or sitting) white plaster figures.

76. Essentially "pop art" in feeling, this arrangement lampoons the conventional, juxtaposing the pristine delicacy of the rose against the withered gnarled statement of the root. A metal ceiling fixture makes the top of the container—another surprise.

87

The question that is continually asked of Pop Art, despite the skill and technique employed by its exponents, is—is it art? Whether or not we feel it is, it implies a point of view that has pervaded our theatre, our book jackets, even our apparel—a willingness to examine small objects and familiar experiences in a close-up, magnified way. Actually we do not see the world around us as continually composed of the most rarified luxurious and glamorous objects — the roses and lilies of other eras. What motion pictures like *The Knack* and *Juliette of the Spirits* do, in the spirit of Surrealism and Pop Art, is stop the camera at some "moment of truth," some setting we have seen in our mind's eye, some familiar detail or some strange one.

To the Pop Artist, texture and form are very important. The roughness of rusty old objects from the garbage heap, the fascinating form of door knobs and locks, automobile parts and springs, the shine of modern metals and the viscosity of globs of paint are all filled with wonder. Motorized sculptures are assembled from hardware, bolts and nuts and jackhammers become knights in full armor.

77. Let's call this arrangement an "ode to a pretzel factory." The forceful maze of wisteria gives an individuality to the design, which includes one tall strelitzia leaf, an aralia leaf, and two clusters of brilliant red geraniums.

PERCEPTION AND
THE ARRANGER

Op Art (or optical art) is the name given another kind of abstraction which can have meaning for the flower arranger. This is painting and sculptural construction which are based on the principles of psychological perception. Here we are involved with the distortions and tricks of the mind in relation to what is seen by the eye. Many Op Art works, for example, use moiré patterns to induce the effects of double vision, the feeling that the piece is moving although one knows it is not.

Light has a great deal to do with the way in which we perceive objects. In Op Art, studies of pegboards in various patterns appear to change depending on where one stands; in other words, illumination changes the surface texture. Similarly, sculptures with voids and indentations appear to be transformed by illumination, and illumination can be used to suggest movement and continuity.

Perception, say the psychologists, is based on our past experience. If we see a series of lines in a certain relationship, our past experience leads us to believe we are looking at a chair, even though we may actually be looking at only a group of wires arranged in a certain manner. Studies in illusion and perception such as the Op Artists have done may well form future concepts for flower arrangers. At the present time, however, it is the concentric circle designs, the wavy lines series, and the basic black, white and primary colors of Op Art that are finding their way into the language of arranging.

Because our world is going through so many rapid changes, art, which is really nothing more than a way of talking about our world, is changing. It's nice to keep up with the rapidly changing vogues in art, like Op, Pop and perhaps next, Glop.

78. Looking at the wavy pattern in the leaves it is easy to imagine that they are moving. This suggests the possibility of creating an "op art" design featuring only croton leaves. Other materials here are bare branches of sumac with wisteria and two chrysanthemums.

89

NEW RULES FOR THE
ADVANCED ARRANGER

But for the interested flower arranger there are a few rules which can be added to the traditional concept of handling nature's beautiful materials so that they now more appropriately fit the most "advanced" taste. The eternal verities of art are still scale, proportion, balance, rhythm, unity, contrast, color and texture. The modern art approach to flower arranging permits much more leeway in the interpretation of these truths.

Early in our discussion, we mentioned such new ideas as "Form Follows Function" and "Less is More." There are other ideas which are basic to modern art. For example:

79. Balance—in this case symmetrical —which is somewhat imperfect gives this design a more endearing quality than if it had been mechanically exact. This imperfection takes on some of the naive quality of primitive art. Materials: One stalk of mullein, dessert spoons, small chrysanthemums, and a modern Japanese container heavily textured with white shellac and grit.

91

80. Contrast — one of the design principles familiar to the traditional flower arranger—is a key to modern work. The intent in this non-realistic flower arrangement is to show linear contrast, the play of straight lines against curved ones. Another facet of abstract design, the absence of a single focus, is also exemplied. Materials: Two strelitzias with one added stem, and a cut philodendron leaf.

1. BE ORIGINAL

The modern art approach to flower arrangement would urge us to make a break with
stereotyped notions. *Be original!* Are there
objects in your life which would appropriately form the basis for a new flower arrangement—perhaps an interesting old tool or uten-
sil, maybe an antique chopper with wooden
handle and half-moon shaped blade of iron;
Japanese glass fishing floats; an embroidered
wall hanging to use as a background; or a
mosaic tile or piece of enamel work your son
made for you at camp which you can use as
a base? Don't ask yourself if it's crazy, but
rather does it have some visual interest—texture, form, color?

81. Well-designed pottery windbells, a
large ceramic container, sun and owl
faces, and triple hanging planter, all
from America House, could inspire
some original flower arrangements.

93

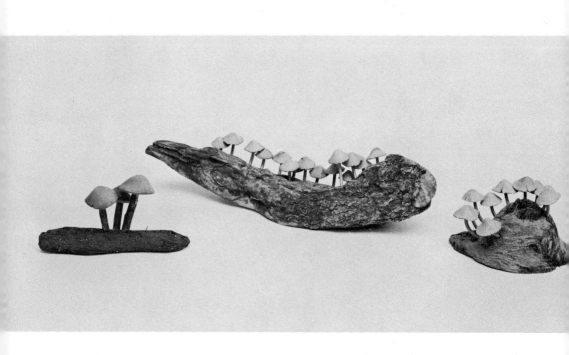

82. Mushrooms, intensely real and precious, are carved of wood and mounted on driftwood by Roger Sloane, and displayed at America House. If you collect driftwood, maybe these miniature carvings will start you on your own way with miniature—but real—plant material.

83. (Opposite) From other forms (this metal one is from America House) could come inspiration for flower arrangements. This rooster seems to be made from windswept leaves and an elongated squash.

84. Opposites, mostly of texture and tone.

2. EXPLORE OPPOSITES

In modern art and design, the flower arranger will find that contrast can be not only exciting but harmonious. Explore the enchantment of opposites — smooth-rough, hard-soft, light-heavy—and texture composition of contrasting natural materials!

85. Another exploration—this one into the size relationships which exist between similar forms (attenuated ovals). The smallest form is echeveria tip and flower, the middle size is the echeveria rosette, and largest ovals are dracaena leaf, looped and up-right, and the container.

3. USE GEOMETRICS

Study geometrical-form characteristics — circles, squares, triangles. Subdivide them with planes and volumes; as an exercise, use combinations of plant materials to fill the cubes of these basic forms. Study the effect of light and shadow on the basic forms.

86. (Opposite) This exercise with triangles and cubes features cattails, an angular container and dried artichokes as well as a dried pothos flower. An abstract work.

4. EXPRESS SPACE-TIME

Remember that ours is a time of new dimensions and relations in space. Consider space in a new way in relation to your arrangement, so that it is *space-time* you are expressing. To express space and time, for example, when using the imagery of the space age, one may use the parabolic curve, as we have noted. This describes the trajectory of a thrown object and measuring it visually gives a sense of emotional participation through time.

Remember that space is just as meaningful in modern composition as is form and color. Empty spaces alternating with full ones have a rhythm of their own.

87. (Opposite) The word parabola comes, in part, from the verb "to throw" so that the form of a parabola is a good choice to express motion, as it does here. An unusual piece of driftwood is set into a round container on one end; the other end is concealed by two large aralia leaves and yellow day lilies.

88. (Opposite) A contrast of line and mass is afforded by this arrangement. Contrast is supplied too by wisteria loops which extend the form of essentially vertical design sideways, forward and backward. A grouping of cattails, loops of wisteria and an aralia leaf with a large chrysanthemum are placed in the opening at the side of the interesting container.

5. USE LINE AND FORM

The flowers and branches of flower arrangements are the lines and forms of sculpture and design in other media. Two fundamental lines dominate our perceptions and actions— the active, vertical line of stretching and growth upward, of falling downward; and the passive, horizontal line of rest and still water. The lines of our composition thus take on either active or passive meaning, restful or energetic, and when they meet at a focal point, create a concentrated energy. They complement, oppose and unite with one another. Through careful planning and spacing in our arrangements we carry the eye of the viewer through to all parts of the composition.

89. Diagonals are lines of restlessness and violence, and the diagonal of the driftwood contributes to the feeling of disquietude aroused in the viewer by this expressive design.

6. CRAFTSMANSHIP TO FOOL-THE-EYE

It is not what you use in your design, so much as how it is put together, that counts. Craftsmanship, good mechanics, makes it possible to use inexpensive materials — tin cans, Styrofoam, lamp bases — to fool-the-eye with paint and texture into believing that materials of weight and importance have been employed.

90. The base looks like stone, but it is a painted block of styrofoam holding inserts of bamboo, one of them used as a seat for a hand-carved whittler.

105

FLOWER ARRANGEMENTS AS A CREATIVE ART EXPRESSION

Modern flower arranging has not only drawn much of its inspiration and theory from contemporary sculpture and painting, it has also gone further towards being a truly creative art in itself. The contemporary arranger is no mere collator of lovely flowers. We are craftsmen in the fullest sense of the word: applying advanced ideas of design, using paint and spray gun, welding materials together, shaping new forms from leaves and plants, bending branches to conform to the demands of modern line, applying surface decorations to add textural interest to our containers. We maintain "libraries" of materials — hardware, fabrics, screening, pottery, plastic sheets, rocks and shells—all to be drawn upon someday.

Like Pop Artists, like the best assemblers and sculptors, we look for materials that suggest something about our world, the passage of time, the hurtling through space, and we look for them everywhere, in city junkyards and shops, on the beaches, in the fields, and in the markets and bazaars of far-off places. But, like the best artists, we too maintain our sense of gaiety and humor. We delight in saying something unexpected and fresh, and we are ruthless in abandoning the old clichés and rules.

91. Let us look for materials that add the ingredient of surprise. With these resplendent copper and brass accessories, a peacock, a rooster, and daisies one could work out many interesting compositions. Courtesy of America House.

107

92. Air filters and driftwood give this arrangement the look of concavity that could suggest a hiding place where orange lilies blossom exotically. Using "found" objects whose original function is so unrelated to flower arrangement gives vitality to our art.

93. The modern arranger's license to create with any new materials is exploited here, with tin roses, and a grouping of mare's tails and osmanthus.

94. In the old way of arranging flowers, the focal point or center of interest was usually placed where the major lines converged, that is, where the plant material entered the container. Modern arrangers decide for themselves whether such treatment is valid for their particular design. Often the answer is yes; in this arrangement, the answer was no. A non-realistic or abstract conception which includes a twisted branch of wisteria, two pine cones raised on stems and a palm boot.

95. Tribal magic is at work here — a mood invoked with loops of baling wire tied to bamboo, aralia leaves, sedum, and a primitive head by Fred Press.

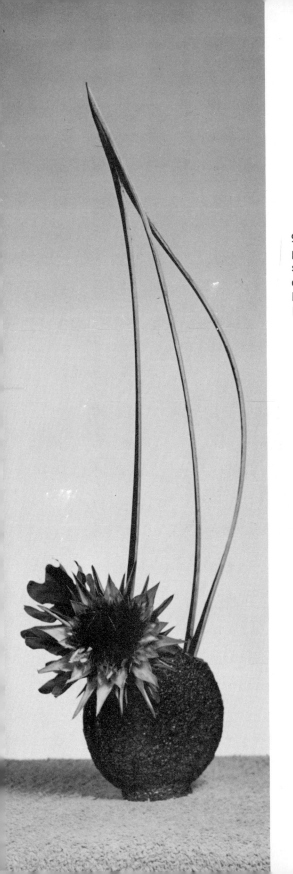

96. Wasteland could be the theme of this composition expressed with a coconut spathe cut in strips and bent into a parabolic curve, and a dessicated artichoke flower in a container is black as charred earth. The green philodendron leaf is expressive of hope.

97. An attenuated diagonal is made from a coconut spathe; three roses and a cut philodendron leaf in a rough black container.

98. Sculpture in natural wood is created with a heavy coconut spathe. It has been bent, cut and painted with aluminum paint, shaded with black, and mounted on a wood block.

99. Two musicians by Fred Press, a rectangle of wrought iron, and red gladioli with an aralia leaf are representative of Lincoln Center.

INDEX

Abstraction, 35, 36, 69, 81, 89, *Plates 2, 3, 5, 13, 15, 25, 50, 67, 68, 69, 86, 94*
  nonrepresentational, 55, 77, *Plates 33, 80*
African carvings, *Plate 25*
Air filter, 35, *Plates 5, 9, 92*
Aluminum, *Plates 6, 7, 11*
America House, *Plates 1, 16, 81-83, 91*
Antelope figurine, *Plate 3*
Anthuriums, *Plate 27*
Aralia, *Plates 8, 11, 12, 14, 21, 28, 34, 35, 48, 56, 72, 77, 87, 88, 95, 99*
Artichoke, *Plates 73, 86*
  flower, 35, *Plates 5, 53, 96*
Aspidistra, *Plate 31*
Assemblages 29, 69-70, 87, *Plates 41, 42, 49, 60, 61, 62, 69*
Aucuba, *Plates 9, 20, 61, 62, 74*

Balance, *Plate 79*
Baling wire, *Plate 95*
Bamboo, *Plates 61, 62, 64, 69, 90, 95*
Banana tree sheaths, *Plate 9*
Batman, 87
Beauty, new concepts of, 19, 73
Bird figurine, *Plates 50, 53, 61*
Boat, *Plate 41*
  container, *Plate 40*
Bog oak, *Plate 4*
"Bottle Dryer," 69
Bowling pin, *Plate 29*
Branches, *Plates 3, 40*
Braque, 69
Brick, *Plate 64*
Brillo packages, 87
Bromeliad, *Plate 55*
Bullfighter and bull figurine, *Plate 38*

Cactus, *Plate 20*
  leaves, *Plates 19, 30, 42*
  spoons, *Plate 15*
Calder, 85, 87, *Plate 74*
Campbell Soup cans, 35
Car spring, *Plate 35*
Carnations, *Plates 20, 38, 56*
Cattails, 70, 73, *Plates 15, 17, 19, 20, 25, 42, 52, 57, 88, 86*
Celosia, *Plate 42*
Center of interest, 36, *Plates 33, 94*
Century plant, *Plate 7*
Chrysanthemums, 81, *Plates 4, 14, 17, 31, 40, 57, 71, 72, 78, 79, 88*
  Fuji, *Plates 11, 18, 30, 62, 74*
Circle designs, concentric, 89

Clock frame, *Plates 49, 61*
Cocoa fiber, *Plate 65*
Coconut spathe, *Plates 8, 12, 13, 22, 23, 28, 34, 38, 53, 71, 96, 97, 98*
Coconut spray, *Plate 4*
Coleridge, *Plate 53*
Color(s), 25, 85, 89, 93, 101
  Impressionistic, 55
  somber, 81
Comic strips, 87
Communication, 59
Composition, 25, 91-105
Concrete, *Plate 7*
Cones, *Plates 63, 94*
Containers, 25, 36, 77, 81, *Plates 1, 16, 81*
  homemade or treated, *Plates 19, 20, 40, 79*
Contemporary Flower Arrangement, 9
Contrast, 97, *Plates 20, 21, 80, 88*
Croton leaves, *Plate 78*
Cubism, *Plates 66, 67*
Cycas palm, *Plate 51*
Cypress knees, 81, *Plate 72*

Dadaism (Dadaists), 61, 69, 87, *Plates 57, 60*
Dahlias, *Plates 3, 7, 10, 21, 26, 35, 48*
Daisies, *Plate 58*
Dali, 61, *Plate 4*
Date spray, *Plate 58*
De Chirico, *Plate 53*
Design principles, 25, 55, 77, 91-105
  traditional, 19, 91, *Plates 2, 3, 6, 15, 33, 45, 50, 59, 94*
Dessert spoons, *Plate 79*
Detail, attention to, *Plate 4*
Diagonals, *Plate 89*
Dieffenbachia, *Plate 10*
Dock, *Plates 3, 4*
Dracaena, *Plates 22, 34, 38, 73, 85*
Dried materials, 69, 81
Driftwood, 69, *Plates 8, 26, 30, 34, 35, 50, 56, 61, 82, 87, 92*
Duchamp, Marcel, 69

Easter arrangement, *Plate 32*
Easter palm, *Plates 55, 56, 59*
Echeveria, *Plates 66, 85*
Emotions, expression of, 75
Energy, 103, *Plate 65*
Environment, response to, 70, 75
Expressionism, 59

Fantastic art, 61
Fantasy, *Plates 53, 56*
Figurines, 69, *Plate 38*
Fish, ceramic, *Plate 55*

Flight symbol, *Plate 61*
Flower show, *Plates 31, 32*
    rules, 9, 36
Focal point, 36, 103, *Plate 94*
Fool-the-eye elements, 105
Force, lines of, 75
Form(s), 35, 88, 93, 101, 103
    basic, 98
    emphasis on, *Plate 67*
"Form follows function," 39, 91
"Found" objects, 35, *Plates 63, 92*
Free-form, 81
Free style, 36
Freud, *Plate 53*
Freudian symbols, 61
Functional parts of an arrangement, 36, 39, *see also* Mechanics
Fungus, 70, *Plates 63, 65*
Futurism, 75, *Plates 39, 65, 66*

Geometric form, 98, *Plate 66*
Geraniums, *Plates 25, 77*
Gladioli, 35, *Plates 15, 50, 99*
Gourds, 70, *Plate 17*
Grapes, fake, *Plate 26*
Gris, Juan, 69

Handbook for Flower Shows, 9, 36, *Plate 60*
Harvest arrangement, *Plate 26*
Hazlitt, 59
History of modern art, 55
Hogarth curve, 75
Honeysuckle, wild, *Plate 63*
Horizontal line, 103
Hosta, *Plate 10*
Humor, 25, 87, *Plates 56, 64*
Hydrangeas, *Plates 6, 54, 65*

Illumination, 89
Illusion, 89
Imagination, 61
Impressionism (Impressionists), 55, 59, *Plate 71*
Indiana, Robert, 69, 70
Iris, *Plates 60, 61*

Japanese rules, 61
Juliette of the Spirits, 88
Junk, 69, 70, *Plate 64*
"Junk culture," 73

Kaffir corn, *Plates 44, 46, 53*
Kale, *Plate 73*
Knack, The, 88

Leger, 25
"Less is more," 51, 91, *Plate 43*
Light, 55, 89, 98
   symbol, *Plate 50*
Lilies, *Plates 13, 26, 28, 32, 34, 92*
   day, *Plates 8, 19, 52, 68, 87*
Lincoln Center, *Plate 99*
Line(s), 25, 35
   of force, 75
   horizontal, 103
   moving, 75
   vertical, 103
Log container, *Plate 63*

Madonna, *Plate 32*
Magnolia, *Plate 60*
Magritte, 61
Mahonia, *Plate 40*
Mare's tails, *Plate 93*
Mass, escape from, 75
Materials, 25, 29, 35, 105
   contrasting, 29
   inspiration from, 51
   "libraries" of, 107
   natural, 97
Mechanics, 36, 39, 105, *Plates 36, 49*
Metal, *Plates 11, 62, 69, 76*
Milkweed pods, 70
Miniatures, *Plate 82*
Mobile(s), 55, 85
Moiré patterns, 89
Mondrian, 25, *Plate 37*
"Moon," 70
Moore, Henry, 85
Motion, 75, 85, *Plates 39, 51, 61, 65, 87*
Mullein, 35, *Plate 5, 22, 48, 59, 60, 79*
Museum of Modern Art, 19
Mushrooms, carved, *Plate 82*

National Council of State Garden Clubs, 9, 36
Nature, inspiration from, 81, 85, *Plates 3, 4, 37*
Negro sculpture, *Plate 25*
Negative values, 73, *see also* Space and Voids
New York Horticultural Society, *Plate 31*
Nostalgic symbols, *Plate 60*
Nonrepresentational abstraction, 55, 77, *Plates 33, 80*

Oleander, *Plates 15, 45*
Onion stalk, *Plate 10*
Op art, 25, 55, 89, *Plate 78*
Opposites, 97, *Plate 84*

Organic forms, 81
Osage oranges, 70, *Plates 22, 45*
Osmanthus, *Plate 93*

Palm boot, *Plate 94*
Palm leaves, *Plate 65*
Palmetto, *Plate 18*
Painted plant material, 105, *Plates 7, 30, 31, 38, 42, 48, 72, 98*
Pampas grass, *Plate 47*
Pandanus fruit, *Plate 49*
Pandanus leaves, *Plate 51*
Parabolic curve, 75, 101, *Plates 87, 96*
Peacock feathers, *Plate 54*
Peony leaves, *Plates 3, 58*
Perception, 36, 89
Philodendron, *Plates 6, 7, 54, 55, 69, 72, 80, 96, 97*
Picasso, 51, 69, 77, 87
Pine cones, *Plate 94*
Plant material
    new treatments of, 77
    spiky, 29, 81
Plow disk, *Plate 49*
Pods, *Plate 63*
Pop art, 25, 29, 55, 87, 88, 107, *Plates 54, 76*
Pothos, *Plate 86*
Precision, *Plate 4*
Press, Fred, *Plates 95, 99*
Primitive elements, *Plates 23, 25, 58, 79*
Primitive head, carved, *Plate 95*
Privet, *Plate 60*
Psychological perception, 89
Purism, *Plate 66*
Purposes of flower arrangement, 25
Pussy willow, *Plates 47, 53*

Radiator mesh, *Plate 18*
Ranunculus, *Plate 59*
"Ready mades," 69
Renoir, 59
Restraint, 51
Rhythm, 101
Rimbaud, *Plate 53*
"Rime of the Ancient Mariner," *Plate 53*
Rooster figurine, *Plate 83*
Root, *Plate 76*
Roses, 35, *Plates 9, 10, 47, 76, 97*
    tin, *Plate 93*
Rules, 59
    for flower shows, 9, 36
    new, 91-105

Scale, *Plate 2*
Scotch broom, *Plates 14, 21, 71*
Sea fan, *Plates 55, 56, 57*
Sea Serpent, *Plate 35*
Sedum, *Plate 95*
Semi-abstraction, *Plate 50*
Sentimental figures, *Plate 3*
Seurat, 59, *Plate 4*
Sloane, Roger, *Plate 82*
Soup cans, 35, 87
Space, 101, *Plates 21, 47, 57*
Space age imagery, 75, 101
Space-time, 101
Spanish theme, *Plates 7, 20, 38, 42*
Speed, expression of, 75, *Plates 51, 65*
Squash, *Plate 73*
Stabile(s), 55, 85, *Plate 74*
Steel bands, *Plate 11*
Steel loops, *Plate 69*
Strelitzia, *Plates 12, 27, 49, 56, 66, 68, 77, 80*
Structural aids, 36, 39
Sumac, *Plate 78*
Sunflower, interpretation of the, *Plate 49*
Surface design, 81
Surprise, 36, 87, *Plates 76, 91*
Surrealism, 25, 61, 87, 88, *Plates 53, 55, 56, 57, 58, 59*
Symbolism, 25

Texture, 29, 35, 81, 88, 93, 97, 105, *Plates 22, 24, 29*
Traditional design elements, *Plates 2, 3, 6, 15, 33, 45, 50, 59, 94*
Turner, 59

Urban materials, 73, *Plate 11*

Van der Rohe, Mies, 39
Vertical line, 103
Voids, *Plates 21, 57*

Wagon wheel, *Plate 60*
Warhol, Andy, 35
Wavy lines, 75, 89, *Plate 78*
Weed holders, *Plate 16*
Weeds, *Plate 17*
Whittler, figurine of, *Plates 4, 90*
Wine bottle, *Plate 9*
Wisteria, *Plates 2, 31, 48, 52, 66, 77, 78, 88, 94*
Wit, 25, 36, 87

Yucca, *Plate 10*